To Rob & A

Alofa

Tusiata x

WILD DOGS UNDER MY SKIRT

TUSIATA AVIA

WILD DOGS UNDER MY SKIRT

Victoria University Press

VICTORIA UNIVERSITY PRESS
Victoria University of Wellington
PO Box 600 Wellington

ISBN -13 978 0 86473 474 7
ISBN-10: 0 86473 474 3
First published 2004
Reprinted 2005, 2012

National Library of New Zealand Cataloguing-in-Publication Data
Avia, Donna Tusiata, 1966-
Wild dogs under my skirt / Tusiata Avia.
ISBN 0-86473-474-3
I. Title.
NZ821.3—dc 22

Published with the assistance of a grant from

ARTS COUNCIL OF NEW ZEALAND TOI AOTEAROA

Printed by PrintStop, Wellington

To Bingo the dog, all my other muses, and to my family and friends

Upu tima'i a le tufuga

Tu'ufau mai oe
O le tu ma le Vavau
Te saga oi eaoe
ae pese a'u.

Advice of the tufuga

It is entirely up to you
this tradition of ancient times
You will groan and weep
I will sing a song.

Contents

Fa'afetai tele lava to: Shannon Welch, Bill Manhire, MA class of 2002, 'Iowa' class of 2003, Fergus Barrowman and the team at VUP, Esther Laban, Noel Faifai, Te Va Gallery

O le pi tautau

A is for Afakasi

A is for afakasi child
left at the crossroads.
Who will save her from the snakes?
Who will save her from the darkness?

E is for Elena

Elena is my aunty's name.
I call her Aunty.
    Eh, suga, you don know nuffing!
    Eh, moe pi, you still piss in da bed!
I have to listen to her because
I am young and don't know about life.

I is for Ipu Ki

    Suga, alu e fai le ipu ki!
Yawning, I shuffle off to the kitchen to make sweet tea and panikeke
I bow my back past the Visitor, the best cups from the cabinet
clinking clinking. The Visitor admires
Aunty's white plastic doilies
and watches me, hungry.

O is for Ola

O is for Ola, the woman who gave me life
is a pa'umuku living somewhere in Apia.
My father was a Palagi. No one knows him.
I should be grateful to be alive to have a good life to live in Niu Sila.
I should be grateful.

U is for Ulu

Aunty says don't leave my hair out
tie it in a knot and don't comb my hair at night-time.
>   *If you comb your hair at night-time bad fings will happen*
>   *da aiku will come an get you!*

F is for Faifeau

Our minister holds his palms up to the congregation.
>   *Lo matou tama e oe le lagi*
>   *save us from the sins of the flesh.*
They are pink like Spam.

G is for Gata

G is for gata
who slips under our door
and winds himself around my legs and squeezes.
Squeezes.

L is for La'u Pele

L is for la'u pele
who will save me from snakes and moe kolo.
He will come like Jesus
he will come like The Rock
he will save me from the baddies.

M is for Moe Kolo

M is for moe kolo
who slips his hard hand under my lavalava.
Aunty snores
he breathes
and slides his finger up.
I watch the darkness.

N is for Niu Sila

I am very lucky.
I can go to the good school
I can get the good education and the good job and help my family.
I am very lucky.

P is for Panty

I hide them under the bed.
Aunty is still sleeping
I lie down and match my breath to hers.

S is for Slut

I know what it means
it means pa'umuku
like my mother.

T is for Teine Lelei

T is for teine lelei
good girl
and T is for teine leaga
bad girl.

V is for Virgin

Mary was a virgin
and God was her husband
but Joseph was her husband
and Jesus was her baby
but Jesus is God.

H is for Herod

H is for Herod who tried to kill the Lord who washed away our sins.
I wash my panty in the shower
wash it with the pulu
wash it with the soap
where did all the blood come from?

K is for Kilikiti

K is for kilikiti at the park
the whole aukalavou, the whole church
is there, Aunty yells and yells at me
Run! Run!
I have the ball but I can't run
my pipi hurts.

R is for The Rock

The Rock picks up the baddy
and holds him over his head
I watch and wait
for the baddy's head to break.

My dog

My dog name is Bingo.
All da dog name is Bingo.
Bingo is da bad dog.
He bite da Palagi mans on da foot.
Aunty Fale throw da big stone to Bingo
and make da sore on Bingo's leg.
Now Bingo walk on da 3 leg.

The Palagi mans he's stay at our house now
and everybody is very happy
specially Aunty who is showing to all da peoples
of our village how we have da Palagi.

Now Bingo no more sleep under da table
because Aunty say he's stink
and no good for da Palagi to smell da stink smell.

Bingo he sleep outside and eat da stone.
Only feed Bingo da stone everytime.
We call
BingoBingoBingo
and throw da stone to him
and laugh
HaHaHa
and da Palagi man shout to us
You kids stop throwing stones at the dog!

And Aunty Fale call us shit and pig
and chase us with da broom and hit us hardhard
on da leg and catch Pela by da hair and shake her
hardhard till Pela's hair is coming out
in Aunty's hand and Pela is cryingscreaming.

We call
BingoBingoBingo
and Bingo come runningrunning
and lick our sore
and grinning.

Return to Paradise

My uncle once broke a man's hands
quietly, like you would snap a biscuit
in half

and then another.
No one knows how loud the man screamed
or if he screamed.

My uncle was Gary Cooper's body double
Return to Paradise, 1952.
He'd studied in Fiji and could speak English

but no one needed him to talk
he was afakasi
and white enough to look white.

Cooper didn't come out much in the day
too hot maybe
they shot him mostly at night

so my uncle stood in the sun for the long shots
in those beachcomber shorts and the hat.
What the villagers remember is the church

where Gary Cooper shoots out the stained glass
windows with a gun.
And the machine that pumped water out of the sea

to make it rain.
The boys remember the cigarettes
and the candy that the crew handed out

all through the night so they would stay
and keep them company.
He was Australian, that man

(most of the crew came from Queensland).
They must have sent him back there
with his broken hands
and his Lucky Strikes.

After Paradise

When the film crews left
and he'd gone long before

for *Boum sur Paris*
one of the house-girls

took to wearing her clothes loose
and sleeping late

fiapalagi they called her
bad example the faletua said.

One of the boys found it
lying in the forest

very small, very white
with strange blue eyes.

Lingua 2

mea: the thing.
fufu: a Nigerian dish.
mea: her cunt.
fufu: to fuck oneself.

fia: want, as in she wants to be a Palagi.
fia mea: as in she wants the *thing* (i.e. to fuck).

What rhymes with Nigeria?

miki: the kissing noise made best by Samoans and / or Nigerians to attract attention / express emotion.

Cafeteria: fale aiga.

fia mea: what does she want?
fale aiga: what does her family want?

miki: to fuck (in _____an)

To find a Nigerian.
To keep herself clean.

Three reasons for sleeping with a white man

tasi

I thought it would be like a border crossing.
I slept with him and dreamt I was sleeping
with him and waking in a room full of children
wearing European shoes.

lua

I thought he might rub off on me.
I slept with him and dreamt he was calling me
his Polynesian Princess

on the wall
the velvet maiden
turns a green shoulder
repositions her hibiscus
and smiles.

tolu

I thought Eh, what the hell
and opened my legs
(not my eyes).

I dreamt I was leaving his house
and all my family were standing outside
my cousin married to her American pilot
my mother
my brother looking like a Maori.
I kissed them all, they kissed me back
even my brother
I asked them
what they were doing.

They asked me
Suga, what are
you
doing?

Shower

(to S.)

That next morning as I stepped from the shower
I caught myself in the mirror, I was shocked
to see the marks like blackened flowers
fallen onto snow, fluttering down the backs of my thighs
like finding something huge and succulent and moving.
I looked closer between my thighs
and on the cheeks of my bottom
and found the purple blooms.

And right then, the way they say people on the verge of death
see their lives flash, I saw him behind me
I saw his hands twisted in black fistfuls, my scalp scorched
my throat curved up like an invitation glistening
to a blade and my mouth open wide
like the death cries of small gods.
I saw him grind me into the bed, the wall
because there was no space no space
between us, he was pushed so far
inside me the room had to give.
I saw his hands on my hips smash me into him
I saw his fingers dig into the flesh
of my ass-cheeks like you would dig
your way through wet sand
if you knew something was buried there –
treasure or a living child.

All I wanted was for him to break
me, split me in half
and then in half again
again and again
until my body was smashed out of existence
like the cliff that becomes
the sand that swims
inside the sea.

Couple

(after Magritte)

The couple with clouds in their heads
are just outlines cut into a wall
so what you're seeing is what's behind

on cloudy days it's clouds
on rainy days water.

Ode to da life

You wan da Ode?
OK, I give you
Here my Ode to da life
Ia, da life is happy an perfek
Everybodys smile, everybodys laugh
Lot of food like Pisupo, Macdonal an Sapasui
Even da dog dey fat
You hear me, suga? Even da dog!

An all da Palagi dey very happy to us
Dey say Hey come over here to Niu Sila
Come an live wif us an eat da ice cream
An watch TV2 evry day
Days of Our Lives evry evry day
Hope an Beau an Roman an Tony De Mera.

Dat how I know my Ode to da life
An also Jesus – I not forget Jesus
He's say to us Now you can
Do anyfing you like
Have da boyfrien, drink da beer
Anyfing, even in front your fadda
An never ever get da hiding
Jus happy an laughing evry time.

Fresh from the Islands

I remember how he would come home
with mangoes smuggled in as palusami

he would hand them over
from his unfamiliar hands.

It was better than Xmas
unwrapping those foreign oranges

from their burnt taro leaf disguises.
He showed us how to cut them

and we took them from him
like grenades

we ran to the backyard to lick the juice
from our arms

and pick the strings from our teeth.
When we came in with our pips

our mother's was untouched –
she was sick

and tired of mangoes.

He lives in Newtown with an Ethiopian

He tells me I am like a virgin
and later soaping myself

I wonder what he meant
tight maybe

like boys
learning their prayers

rocking back and forth
back and forth over their holy books

chanting
God is Great. God is Great.

When I ask him if he will take me
to meet his Ethiopian flatmate

the answer is No, for he may rob you
like rice from the desert.

I say cunt
in my head

so loudly
the Ethiopian salivates.

Evil Mr Golliwog
stay away from the rice flower girl.

I mistake the beating
of my heart

for the sounds of his footfalls
from Rintoul Street

all the way across Ru'bal Khali
to the Red Sea.

I want him to speak to me in clichés
heaps of them, piled around me like gold

coins stamped with the image of the Prophet
made of tin-foil and chocolate.

I say I'll let you wear me
like a coat made of some flayed

animal, something inside out
you can run your hands over my flesh

and read my sparkling entrails
for what is the point of a skin.

Meat

I said nothing at the wedding
even the flowers ate each other.

Weddings in the sand are like that
people concerned about their hands

how well painted they are.
I wanted mine black, no pattern.

People concerned about the food
how to lead it home over the dunes.

I never wanted to eat again.
Ever.

The goats and I understood each other
and apart from the bells

would leave this place to ululation
and the sound of meat.

Vasega: Da Revolution Is Coming

Missionary: This is a picture of a basket.
                 What is this?
Children: Dis ees a peekcha of a pasket.
Missionary: This is a basket.
                 What is this?
Children: Dis ees a peekcha of a pasket.
Missionary: **This is a basket.**
                 What is this?

DIS EES A PEEKCHA OF A PASKET.

Pa'u-stina

I am da devil pa'umuku kirl
I walk down da street shakeshake my susu
I chew gum an smile wif my gold teef flashing
I call out to da good womens
sitting sitting in deir house
Eh, ai kae! An I make dem see my arse.

I am da dog kirl wif da fire in my arse
Dey call me da woman not da kirl
My thighs rub together make da fire in deir house
My fat taro legs my fat taro belly my fat taro susu
I walk pas all da good womens
An I laugh wif my white teef flashing.

I smell like da hot rain flashing
An all da good mens are looking for my arse
All da good mens are waiting for da back of deir womens
You are da good kirl da sexy kirl da lovelybeautiful kirl
Dey run like da dog I let dem lick my susu
Dey run in da back dey run to deir house.

I walk pas da high cheif' house
I walk on da high-heel shoe like da spear flashingflashing
My bra tighttight so I have da 4 susu
Da whole cheif' council look for my arse
An make da special fine for da pa'umuku kirl
I can hear da laughinglaughing da smiling of da womens.

My red toenails wavewave to da womens
My red toenails shineshine to da womens in deir house
I am da devil pa'umuku kirl
An I laugh when dey fine me wif my red lips flashing
I pull my skirt up an show my fat taro arse
I laugh like da dog da volcano shake my susu.

I am drinking on da road and playing wif my susu
Dancing wif da dogmen running from deir womens
I am laughing at da dogmen licking at my arse
I am laughing at da dogmen away from deir house
I am laughing at da dogmen deir black arses flashing
We love you sexy kirl we love you beautiful kirl we love you lovely kirl.

I laugh like da dog like da volcano like da arse hole. Dey cry for me like susu
We want you hot rain kirl we have forgotten our womens
We will go to da house of Pulotu we will go wif our black arses flashing.

My first time in Samoa

Our passport photos
mine: purple lipstick
my sister's: thin thin eyebrows
like bad surprises.

The heat of course
that was the first thing
and the smell
wet like semen.

They picked us up from the airport
in a truck. We sat, wind cooling our sweat
and watched houses with no walls pass by.

We looked in at pyramids
of tinned corned beef
stacked on shelves
Hey, what are they?
Shops they said.

We scratched in the village
too hot
too stink
we hated going to the toilet
our legs bled.

If you could choose
would you rather stay here for a whole year
or sleep with . . .
Mr Muldoon?

Apia
Tusitala Hotel Bar
New Year's Eve.
10 gin and lemonades
puked up in the potted palms
unconscious on a deckchair
while our cousin tried to get into my sister's pants.

What about this one then
would you rather stay here for six months
or marry . . .
a Samoan?

I dreamt about him before I met him

He leaves me early
and after a while I realise
I'm still burning
a towel jammed
between my legs
my fingers and feet on fire.

I carry him round inside me
like blood
the kind that tells you
you're sick.

Why is this the part I love the best
the moment before treachery
the bit just before his hands are on me.

I am a series of spasms
shining like a giant centipede
macheted into pieces
each section thrashing free
of the other.

I am a speared bonito
red on silver on red.
I am the orange orange papaya
spurting into the black
mouths of a hundred sated bats.

Brutaweet

That day in the woods when they stopped the car
and fucked

that was early on, you'd expect that kind of thing
to burn down to something steady
that would cook things like pies

but for her nothing changed, she continued
to scorch like a saint.

Even in her dreams nothing slakes her
so she chooses the company of dragons

big black ones with gold teeth and cigarette smoke
and shiny hard chests.

She climbs a tree and watches
like Brutaweet the Ethiopian maiden

as Afro George drives
a spear right through that scaled flaming heart.

Teine

I tol you before I'm da real kirl and dis my real hair
when I live in Aussie it's down my muli
so I can sit on it an all da man
dey like it too too much
I don care what anybody fink – I make a lot a money
in dat place – all gone now
my dear but I make a lot a money
in dat place.
You hear bout dat place in Pago Pago?
da Saiga man Li Fang or somefing like dat
he run it – call da Red Door every
body know – near da tuna factory stink
like da fish – he bring da kirls from here
kuā-back kirls don know nuffing
fink dey work in da hotel. Stupid.
Now dey all send back to deir village
in kuā with nuffing
poor fing. Anyway Li Fang
run away maybe here fucken Saiga
his wife a Samoa too – bloody
bitch I like give her a hiding if I see her.

Tamaiti

My family have a hundred curses:
I'll smack your head
with the chair
your teeth will roll
on the floor.

Fale lines up the children
when visitors come.
What's my name?
My name is cow shit
dog shit piss in the bed shit
my sister is the shit of pigs.

Fale hits the kids with the broom.
What are you smiling for?
Break your mouf
break your bones
cook you in da oven.

The kids are good at looking blank
they shake their heads at lollies
but when Uncle Tavita brings them boxing gloves
from New Zealand
they leap and run like chickens.

Girls' life

Aunty Fale explains about the Girls' Life
If you drink beer dat means you are da bad kirl
and you are looking for da boy.
Smoking is the same.
Children Respect Your Parents.

Everyone knows Fale's kids have four different fathers
it cost her parents in fines to the village:
6 pigs 4 fine mats 2 boxes of corned beef and money
every time.

In '73 she went to New Zealand
worked at Kiwi Bacon
spoke English
but her sisters told her
Go back
look after our parents.
We have husbands, children here
Go back.

You have da baby – you stay home.
Look after da kids
pick up da coconuts
feed da pigs
da in-laws.

Fale has sixteen grandchildren
six in New Zealand
she doesn't beat them as much
as she beat her own kids.

Pela, the youngest
stops crying
as soon as Grandma
looks her way
straight away.

Fings da kirls should know

Don hang your panty outside.
Don forget to wash your panty in da shower
otherwise da ants will come an eat da dirty.
Don use da same towel as da boy.
Don comb your hair in da night-time.
Don wear your hair out.
Don show your shoulder.
Don wear da trouser
except in da town.
Don swim on da Sunday.
Don play on da Sunday.
Better you don do nuffing on da Sunday
just go to da church, stay home an go to sleep.
Don sleep in da lavalava only.
Don sleep by yourself.
Don walk by yourself specially in da dark.
Don forget to cover da mirror at da night-time.
Don answer back.
Don be da show off.
Don kaukalaikiki.
Don fiapoko.
Don kafaovale – don make aroun.
Don make da frien wif da boy.
Don make da bad fing wif da boy.
Don drink or smoke or go to da night club.
Ua e loa? I said, don you drink or smoke or go to da night club!

Remember, kirls, obey your parents, den you will live long in da land.

Who loves who more?

Watching pigs die like white explosions
making ovens underground to cook
all the ones you hate
all people whose legs remind you of yams
whose ribs stick out like dogs'.

My aunty is as cruel as three years of spiders.
If a child passes she grabs it by the hair and shakes it
till it folds its arms and legs
like a little Buddha.

Kisses are not a question.
Children massage her feet
and don't look up during prayers.

She's hard because she's hard.
Her own sister wants to disappear.
That's what family meetings are for
that and making fun of the children.

13th October 1979

Today was our first real summer day.
Summer just has to be good.

Got to get a good report
and a boyfriend.

I'd better start pulling up my socks.
In nine days it's M's birthday

better get her a present.
It's good to have a best friend.

Mum moved into my bedroom
about two weeks ago now.

I've gotta get a lock on my door
I spose I forgot to say

Mum and Dad are separating soon.
There are lots of reasons why

one of them is Mum's a lesbian.
Today I went to Brighton

and got my ears pierced for the third time.
That makes six holes now.

Looming

I call it my looming
dread, like the mornings I wake
crying quietly at the grey
in my room, like whispering to my sleeping
mother – do I *have* to
like the short cuts I can't take
like the standing outside not breathing
like my hand on the doorknob
counting to twenty and twenty
and twenty.

Cheek

The crash comes
and I fly from the top bunk

along the hallway to the lounge
my feet not feeling the floor

and there they are
my father's hand

on my mother's white
throat. Call the police

like soprano
me slow dancing

toward the receiver
my father's hand stretched out

clasping me like you clasp the cheek
of an irresistible child

pulling me across the carpet
like a cutie.

Fa'afetai mo mea ai

Everyone eats up to their elbows
we are direct descendants of flesh-eaters.

Try ripping apart a steaming pig and tell me
that doesn't feel good.

There's a reason for all the grease
and who cares if we are fat

huge
and the noises we make

swallowing the dead.
The pigs scour outside

the dogs dribble inside
if we smell them we kick them

the cats screech like shadows.
People on the road

the dogs run to rip them to pieces.
Bring us a bowl of water

a cloth
to wash our hands.

Ifoga: to Helen Clark

In the old days, Helen
you would have presented yourself trussed

like a pig
ready for umu

we might have sat
with our backs turned all day

going about our business
eating working shitting

while the sun glazed
you pink

laughing sleeping pissing
while you held your joints

stiff and then, Helen
if we decided

not to kill
you, cook

you
then

you could consider yourself
forgiven.

Samoans are known for their hospitality

We go with my brother
and his wife to McDonald's Apia

because it is cool
and Samoa is far too hot for them, especially the wife

who is not quite in a state of shock
but probably will be soon.

They sit down and say it is usually against their ethics
to eat at McDonald's

Did you see what they gave us for breakfast this morning!
What was it anyway?

They sit down opposite Dad and me
and order

2 Big Macs
2 Large Fries
2 Large Cokes
2 Chocolate Sundaes

and they eat them
telling Dad and me

it cost twenty-eight tala and fifty sene
which is about twenty dollars New Zealand

which is still really expensive
by any standard.

Dad and I sit there and listen
even though some of what they say is muffled by fries.

They become matai

Saofa'i / The Investiture

Someone tells him
that they are saying
there are important things to consider.
He's heard this is the streamlined version
of the old way:
the hanks of coloured material around his waist
stand in for ie toga.
The learnt speech is stiff on his lips
like Latin.
Someone (his sister?) says this new way
is a good way – cheaper – no food, no fine mats
less pressure on the family.
She wears ie toga though
pounds of it.

Lauga / The Oratory

The words rise like the souls of birds.
He can't trace their flight
but feels them brush his ears
their rush and wheel.
The odd one catches him
in the shape of a familiar object
sun, man, dog
in the shape of a well known god
Tangaroa / Tagaloa
in the shape of a hero he's read about
in a missionary book.

Feagaiga / The Covenant

There are things he recognises
the taupou
the kava
the passing of the cup
the fact that his sister
has her speech written on the inside of her wrist.

I arrive again

I arrive again and they all kiss me.
I kiss them back.
Everyone has grown up or down.

Pela has cut her hair
the great aunt I am named for is still sitting on the concrete
even after all these years

and hauls herself to hands and knees.
I am worried about her wrinkled shins.
The mosquitoes remind me my skin

is as sweet as the Sky Breakers'
and ripening like guava.
Someone will bring me salve.

All my cousins are here
and wearing uniforms:

United States Army
Qantas
WINZ.

Waiting for my brother

I kill wasps
between copies of *Samoan Custom*
and *Flotsam and Jetsam from the Pacific Ocean.*

There is a line of the dead
above my head as I sleep.
My brother will have to
make his own arrangements.

Village princess

My sister was a taupou
so when our parents gave up
caring whether I'd ruined myself
she was still climbing out the windows
at 28.

Our cousin gave up her long golden hair
for my sister's headdress.
She was beautiful dancing
her pale brown arms oiled
and us, a thousand
glinting in her mirrored forehead.

She ran away to Colorado
with a white guy called Randell.
She got herself a scholarship
and a job as a body-piercer.

No one talks about titles now
or going to Amerika.

Helicopter

My mother told him
With all that money you could have bought a helicopter.
You could have packed them all in
      Cousins like corned beef
      Aunties like elegi
      Uncles like saimigi
      Brothers like taro
      Sisters like cabinbread
      Nephews like bananas.
And you could've packed us in
a big car, a big house, the best school
a marriage that would've worked like the best
the most American helicopter in the world.

Susu

Dis da true story. Malia she fa'asusu da baby an da milk it run down on da floor
das why da whole place is white colour an call *Grotto of da Milk*
dat mean da church of da milk an dat one in Ierusalema
I know coz our Aunty Teresa da kaupou sa an been to Ierusalema
even she seen Jesus dere coz dat where he live
– you don know dat, den you don know nuffing!

You know what for dat church?
for make da womens have da baby
just you go dere and on your knee an ask to Malia for anyfing you wan it
like da baby or da susu come out if is stuck
anyfing like dat.

Da other day Mele she come home an she not say anyfing
she just have da shower an do da saka an go to bed
she don even wan eat her fav'rit kale pisupo
we fink she angry to someone
we don even know she have da baby in her stomach dat time
we eat da whole lot kale pisupo coz is our fav'rit too.

Sefa da name of da boy make da pregnant to Mele
he come wif his whole aiga
an make da apologise
bring da pig an da pusa apa pisupo an da big money
we saying why his aiga make dose fing?
an our other cousin tell us is becoz Sefa make da rape to Mele
an now we remember dat day for da kale pisupo.

When da baby he borned Mele's susu get bigger an bigger
even she look so funny to us
but she just cry an cry an don wan fa'asusu da baby
so we buy da susu in da packet from da supamakit
an use da bottle for fa'asusu da baby.
Da baby we name him Ierusalema
is da nice name for da baby, ah?

Photo: Epifania

Baby held like an aeroplane.
Epi has no head.
Her legs are crossed with centipedes.
Paulo in the background.
Paulo sitting on the sofa
Looking at the camera.
Paulo puts his head back
And like that he looks dead.
Epi holds the baby.
Crosses on the backs of her knees
Iesu on the wall
Either side of the mirror.
Baby's dressed in yellow.
Paulo's not moving.
Ulas round the photos.
Iesu on the cross.
Her fingernails are short and dirty.
Baby dressed in yellow.
Epi's legs.
Epi's baby.
Epi's husband.
Epi's living room.
This is about Epi's
Malu.
The story goes like this
Taema and Tilafaiga
Were Samoan Siamese twins
Joined at the hip
They swam to Samoa singing

Tattoo the women and not the men
Tattoo the women and not the men.
This is not about Paulo.
This is not about the Master.
The twins they forgot
The words
They fucked it up
The words
Tattoo the men not the women
Tattoo the men not the women.
This is about Epi.
She is in front.
This is about her
Malu.
This is how it ended
Men got the pe'a.
Epi holding the baby.
Iesu looking on.
Paulo shaped like a cross.
All of us looking on.

Frame

The video arrives from America
Return to Paradise 1952
Gary Cooper, Roberta Haines
Thanks expressed to the people
of Matautu, Lefaga.

I try to see them all, keep them
my father's father
church scene, centre front
the long dead aunt beside him
great or great-great.

33 minutes in and I find him –
the big house burns, the children tie tin cans
to the wardens and watch them run –
the villagers have revolted
and returned to their free loving ways.

He takes the hand of a dusky maiden
I make them run frame by frame
into the bushes.
Roberta dances and beckons to Gary
she moves her hands like a real Samoan.

My dad spends half a century in the bushes.
He doesn't know they're supposed to be
making love under the coconut trees.
He thinks they're running from the curfew.

I know he had enough English to tell the others
what to do, how to connect the cables
where to move the generator
but he still thinks he and Tupe
the district nurse were fleeing

he doesn't know
about the revolution.
He thinks it was a fiafia.

Alofa

Alofa go for da walk . . . walking walking Alofa find alofa everywhere in da bush in da tree under da bush under da tree in da dark alofa . . . plenty alofa in da dark.

Alofa go to church . . . Alofa singing to Jesus Alofa praying to Jesus . . . Jesus bring me plenty alofa plenty money too Jesus make me win da bingo den I make da big donation show my alofa to all da peoples in da church an show my alofa to da faifeau too an everybodys say Alofa is da good kirl – she got so much alofa.

Jesus love Alofa so Alofa win da bingo.

Alofa go to Apia . . . eating icecream eating pagikeke eating keke pua'a . . . alofa on her fingers alofa on her shining shining lips Alofa smiling to all da peoples Alofa smiling to all da boys especially all da mens especially.

And when da night is coming Alofa smell like da frangipani like da moso'oi like da Impulse perfume come from Niu Sila and so many boys so many mens Love Alofa
Love Alofa Love Alofa.

Alofa dancing in da Tropicana nightclub . . . all da fa'afafine watching to Alofa – Tisha, Sindy, Leilani, Tia, Lamay, Devinia – all da fa'afafine making like da real kirls making da jealous (no alofa no alofa only jealous) Alofa don't even care Alofa don't even look Alofa twirling on da dance floor showing her alofa to da Palagi mans showing her alofa to da Samoan mans.

Alofa making alofa in da Seaside Inn with da Palagi man name Bruce . . . Alofa singing and singing in da Seaside Inn in da dark Alofa singing . . . Alofa ia te oe Bruce. Alofa ia te oe.

Alofa on da bus – Pacific Destiny Bus – da bus to Alofa's village in da kuā-back . . . Jesus hanging in da bus hanging from da mirror in da bus watching Alofa all da way to home . . . Fea lou alofa Alofa? Fea lou alofa?

Da father of Alofa send her to da faifeau (who is also da uncle of Alofa) . . . da faifeau make her da black eye an da big lip an da fula on her maka in front all da peoples . . . Alofa you make us ashame. Alofa you make us want to throw you to da shark. Alofa you are da pig-kirl. Alofa you are da pa'umuku kirl.

Long time an Alofa get up early Alofa go for da walk . . . Alofa walking far far to da bush and lie down under da tree . . . Alofa is crying an crying Alofa is screaming an screaming Alofa is holding an holding her stomach an da blood is coming an coming . . . an when it's finish – Alofa call it Alofa too.

Avia

(*in memory of Le Mamea Simanu'a Avia Esera*)

You didn't die on the road to Apia
when the soldiers opened fire
you hit the ground with your trumpet
you hid in the bushes in Lefaga
and your wife told them you were gone.

There were other times you didn't die
that no one has told me about.

You said everyone
was to wear white at your funeral
your eldest son wore a jacket
that he got from the freezing works.
No one knew that but me.

There was a line of men
almost as far as I could see
they stood before you one by one
and lay down a coconut leaf
the tulafale wove them into the air
to help us remember Polualeuligana
and how he saved us from ourselves.

The women washed you and talked to you
like you were still alive
and when they left
there was that moment
when it was just you and me.
I wanted you left like that
in skin and pe'a.

Wild Dogs Under My Skirt

I want to tattoo my legs.
Not blue or green
but black.

I want to sit opposite the tufuga
and know he means me pain.
I want him to bring out his chisel
and hammer
and strike my thighs
the whole circumference of them
like walking right round the world
like paddling across the whole Pacific
in a log
knowing that once you've pushed off
loaded the dogs on board
there's no looking back now, Bingo.

I want my legs as sharp as dogs' teeth
wild dogs
wild Samoan dogs
the mangy kind that bite strangers.

I want my legs like octopus
black octopus
that catch rats and eat them.

I even want my legs like centipedes
the black ones
that sting and swell for weeks.

And when it's done
I want the tufuga
to sit back and know they're not his
they never were

I want to frighten my lovers
let them sit across from me
and whistle through their teeth.

Notes

O le pi tautau

The Rock (aka Rocky Maivia / Dwayne Johnson) is a Samoan / American WWF wrestler.

Brutaweet

'Brutaweet' is from the Ethiopian version of the story of St George and the Dragon. Brutaweet was the name of the maiden St George rescued.

Fings da kirls should know

The last line is from a bible verse often quoted to children.

I arrive again

Sky Breakers: the literal translation of Palagi – *pa*: to break, *lagi*: sky. When Palagi first arrived in Samoa in their boats, they 'broke' the sky / horizon.

Photo: Epifania

'Photo: Epifania' is from a photo by Mark Adams of Epifania (Epi) Suluape, wife of Samoan tattoo master, the late Su'a Suluape Paulo II. Paulo died at Epi's hand in 1999.

Centipedes are a common Samoan tattoo pattern.

Avia

In memory of my grandfather, Le Mamea Simanu'a Avia Esera, who among other things was a member of the Mau, the Samoan resistance movement against New Zealand's administration of Samoa in the early 1900s.

The first stanza refers to a peaceful protest of the Mau, now known as Black Saturday. In this instance the New Zealand army opened fire on protesters on the road to Apia killing several of them.

The third stanza refers to the story of Polualeuligana, who was the son of Malietoa, a powerful chief of Samoa. Malietoa practised cannibalism, demanding that a pair of young people be brought to him regularly for him to dine on. One day on the beach Polualeuligana heard the pitiful cries of two people in distress. When he asked them why they were crying they explained they were to be Malietoa's dinner the next night. Polualeuligana asked them to weave him into a coconut leaf food basket and then had himself presented to his father. When the basket was laid in front of Malietoa and he opened it up, Polualeuligana's point was made. Malietoa then called an end to cannibalism in Samoa.

Wild Dogs Under My Skirt

The fourth stanza refers to the traditional Samoan story of the octopus and the rat. The rat tricked the octopus into letting him ride on his head from one island to another. During the free ride the rat shit on the octopus' head.

Glossary

Note: I have used both 't' and 'k' styles of Samoan.

afakasi: half-caste

ai kae: eat shit

aiga: family / extended family

aiku: spirit, demon

Alofa ia te oe: I love you

alofa: love / a name

aukalavou: youth group

elegi: tinned herring

Epifania: epiphany / a name

Fa'afetai mo mea ai: Thank you for the food

fa'afafine: (literally) to be like a woman, a biological male who takes the roles of a female – this can cover a range of sexual identities, from drag queen to transsexual and beyond

fa'asusu: breast feed

faifeau: minister

faletua: minister's wife

Fea lou alofa?: Where is your love?

fiapalagi: want to be like a Palagi

fiapoko: know-it-all

fiafia: celebration

fula: swelling

gata: snake

ie toga: fine mats, used for ceremonial purposes

Ierusalema: Jerusalem

Iesu: Jesus

ifoga: apology

ipu ki: cup of tea

kafaovale: a person who goes out partying a lot

kale pisupo: curried tinned corned beef

kaukualakiki: cheeky

kaupou sa: nun

kava: ceremonial drink made from the ava plant

keke pua'a: pork bun

kilikiti: Samoan cricket

kuā / kuā-back: remote villages

la'u pele: my dear one

Lo matou tama e oe le lagi: Our father in Heaven

maka: eye

Malia: (Virgin) Mary

malu: female tattoo from upper thigh to lower knee, sometimes also on the pubic area

matai: titled person, chief

Mele: Mary

misa: fight / argument

moe kolo: a man who creeps at night / molester

moe pi: bed-wetter

moso'oi: scented flower

muli: bottom

Niu Sila: New Zealand

O le pi tautau: Samoan alphabet, usually in the form of a chart with pictures

ola: life / a person's name

pa'umuku: slut / prostitute

pagikeke: pancake

Palagi: white person

palauvale: swear

palusami: cooked balls of coconut cream wrapped in taro leaves – allowed into New Zealand from Samoa because they are cooked

panikeke: pancakes

pe'a: male tattoo from mid-abdomen to lower knee

pipi: vagina

pisupo: corned beef

Pulotu: Samoan underworld

pulu: coconut husk fibre used for washing

pusa apa pisupo: box of canned corn beef

Saiga: Chinese

saimigi: instant noodles

saka: cooking – boiled food, often taro

sapasui: chopsuey

Sefa: shortened version of Iosefa, i.e. Joseph

Suga, alu e fai le ipu ki: (to a girl) Go and make a cup of tea

suga: form of address to a woman / girl (colloquial)

susu: milk / breasts

tamaiti: children

taupou: the one who makes the kava during the ceremony / virgin, titled, unmarried young woman who holds a ceremonial position in the village

teine leaga: bad girl

teine lelei: good girl

tufuga: master tattoo maker

tulafale: orator / talking chief

Ua e loa?: Do you understand?

ula: lei, shell or flower necklace

ulu: hair

umu: Samoan earth oven

vasega: class, also body of people